Country Cottages Coloring Book

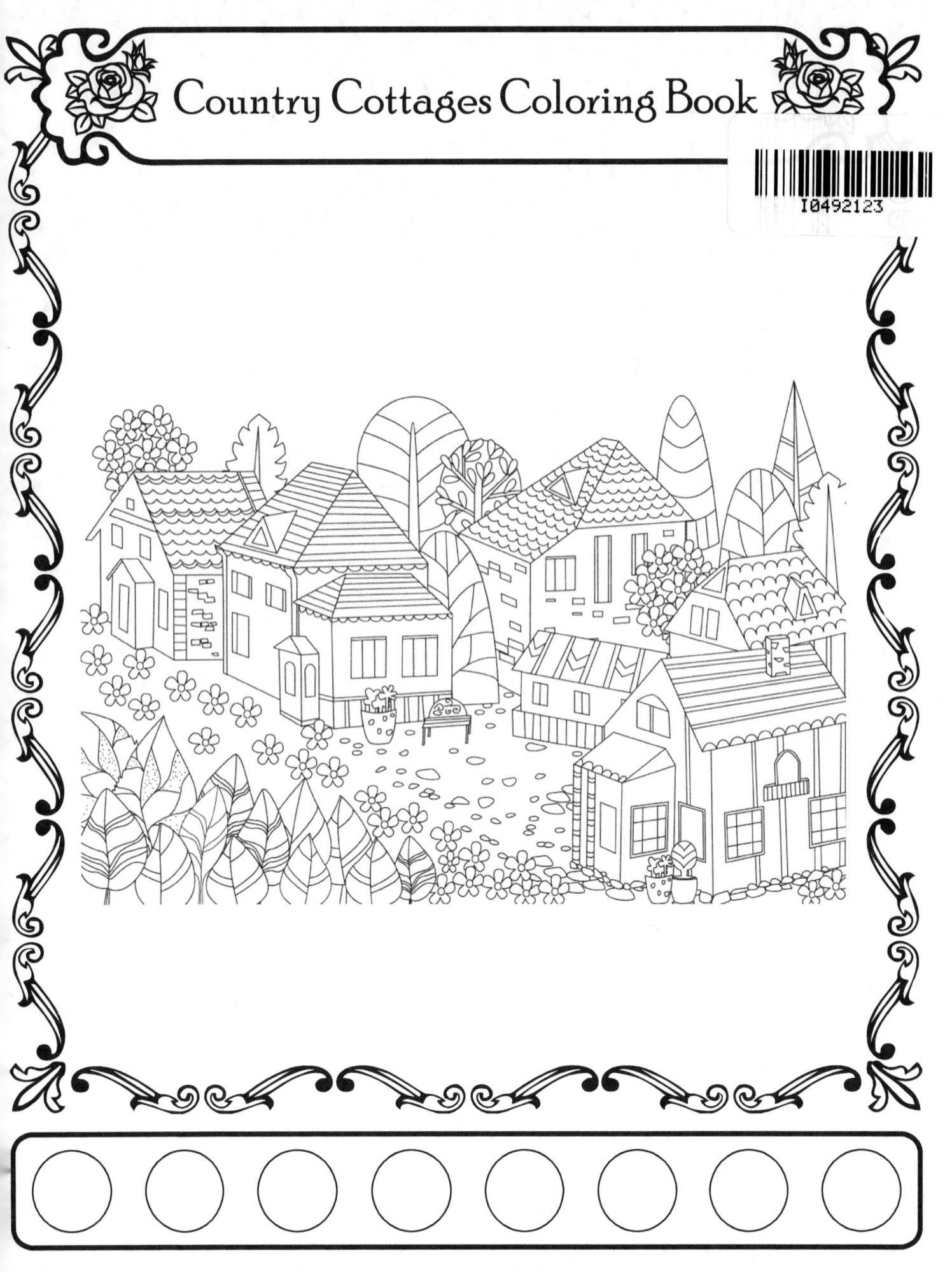

Country Cottages Coloring Book

Country Cottages Coloring Book

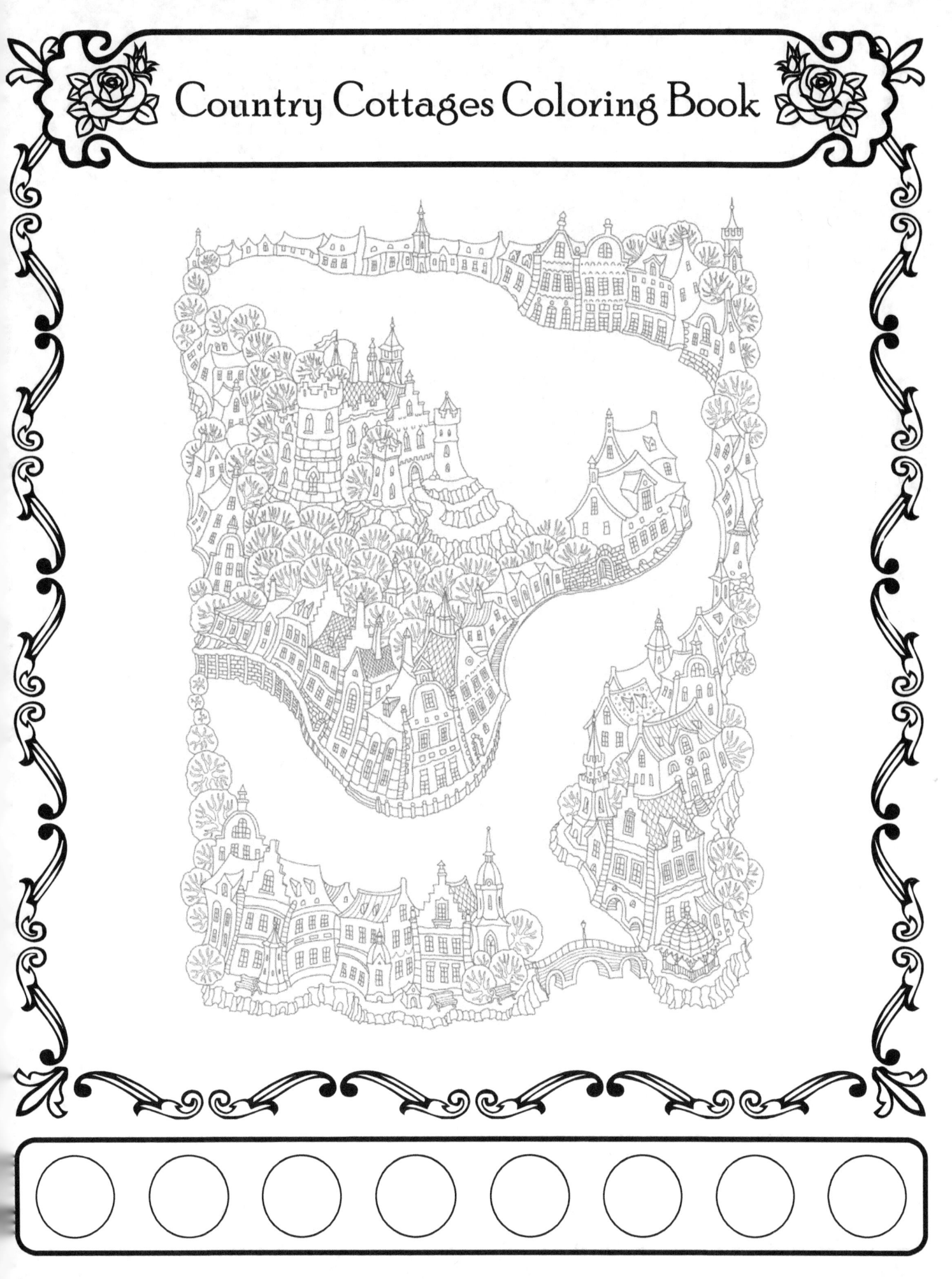

Country Cottages Coloring Book

Country Cottages Coloring Book

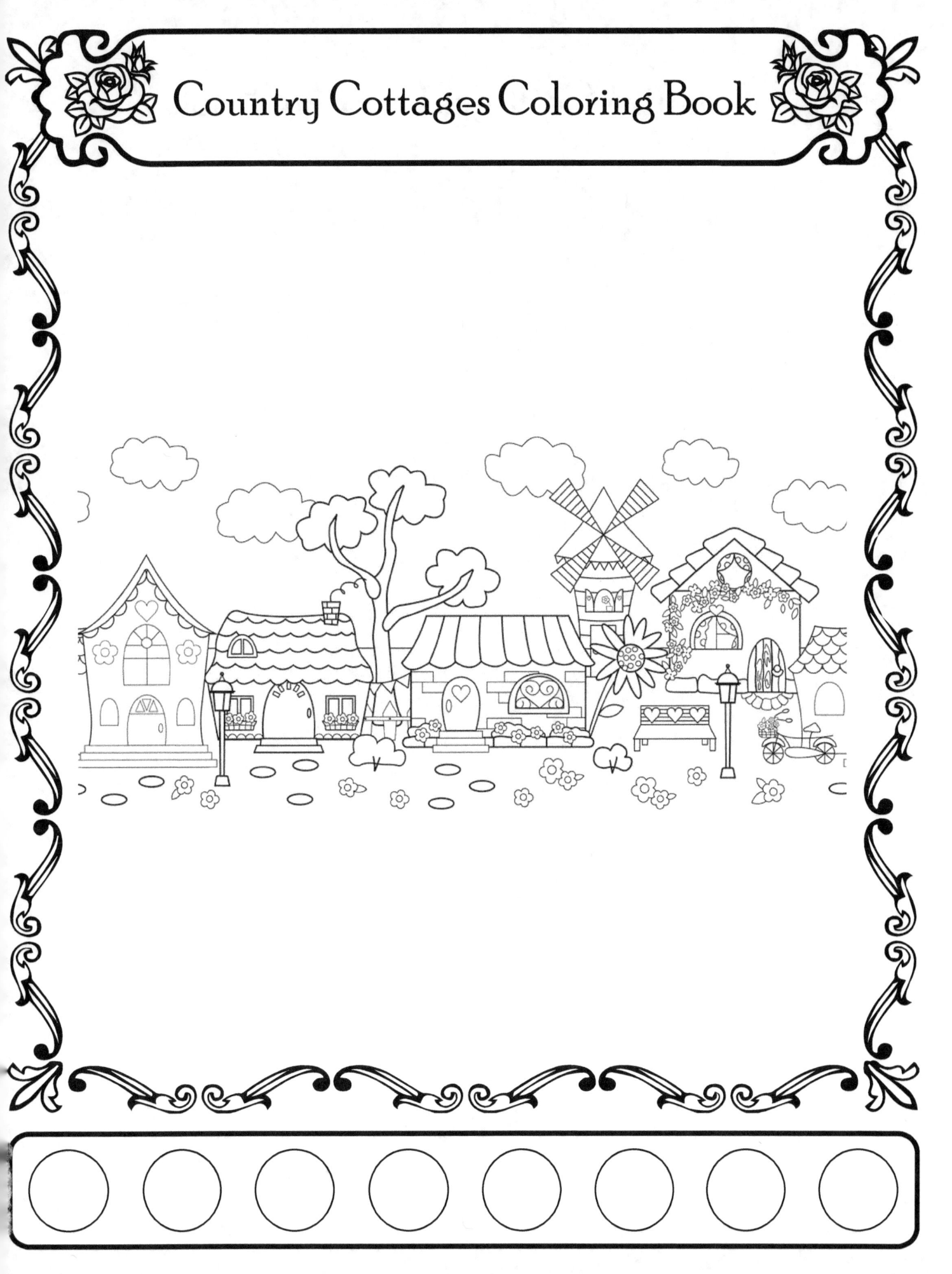

Country Cottages Coloring Book

Country Cottages Coloring Book

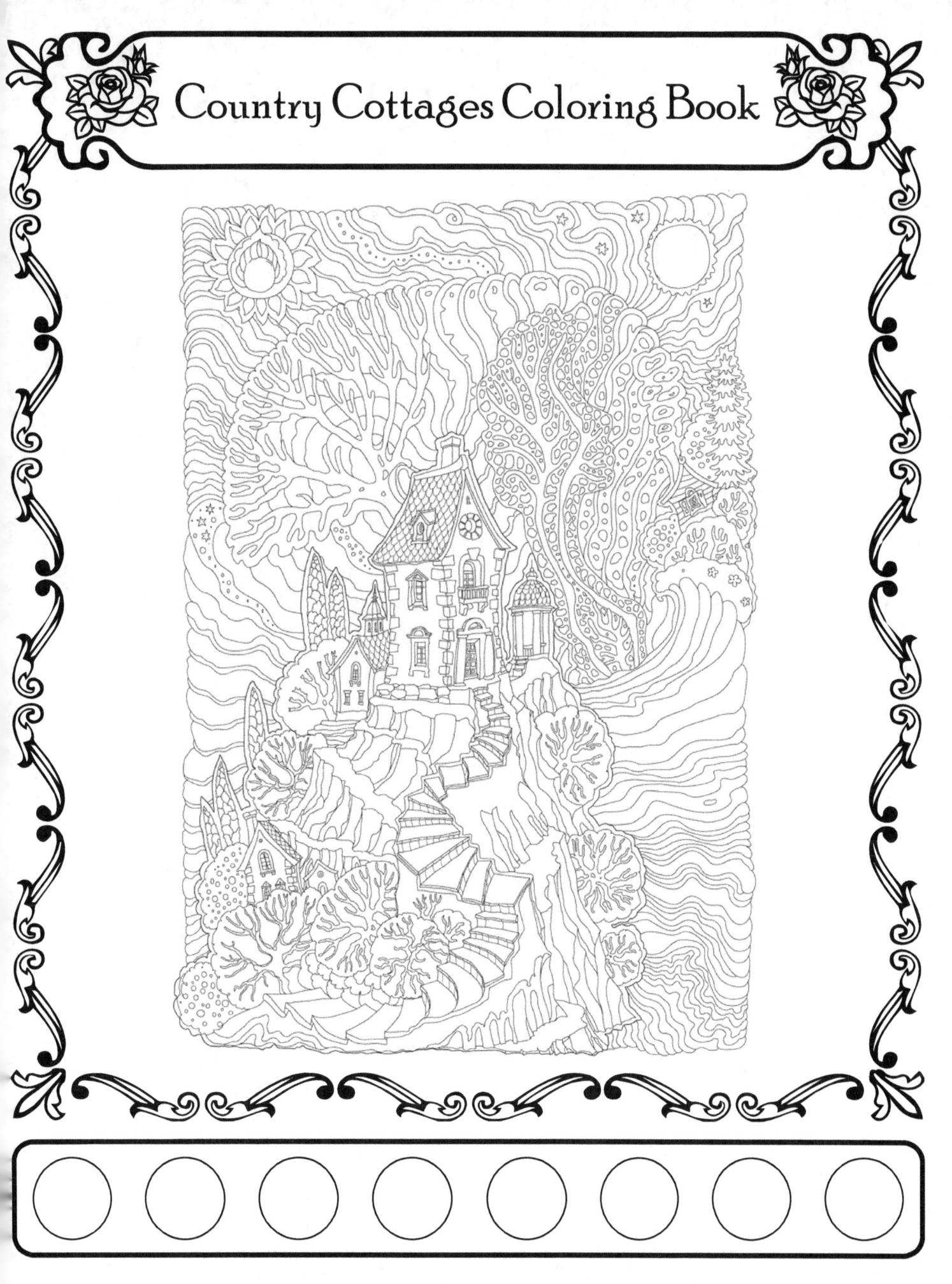

Country Cottages Coloring Book

Country Cottages Coloring Book

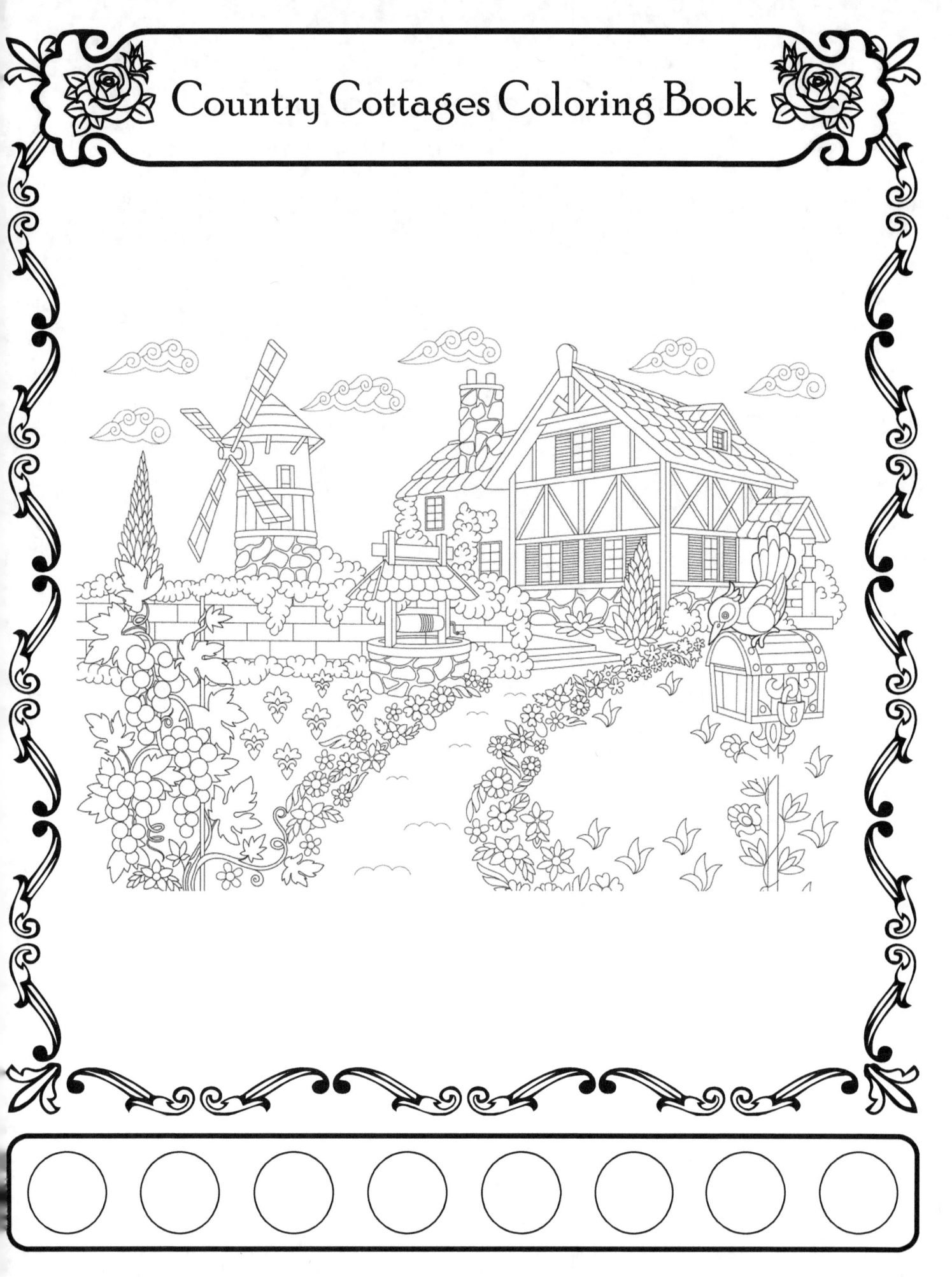

Country Cottages Coloring Book

Country Cottages Coloring Book

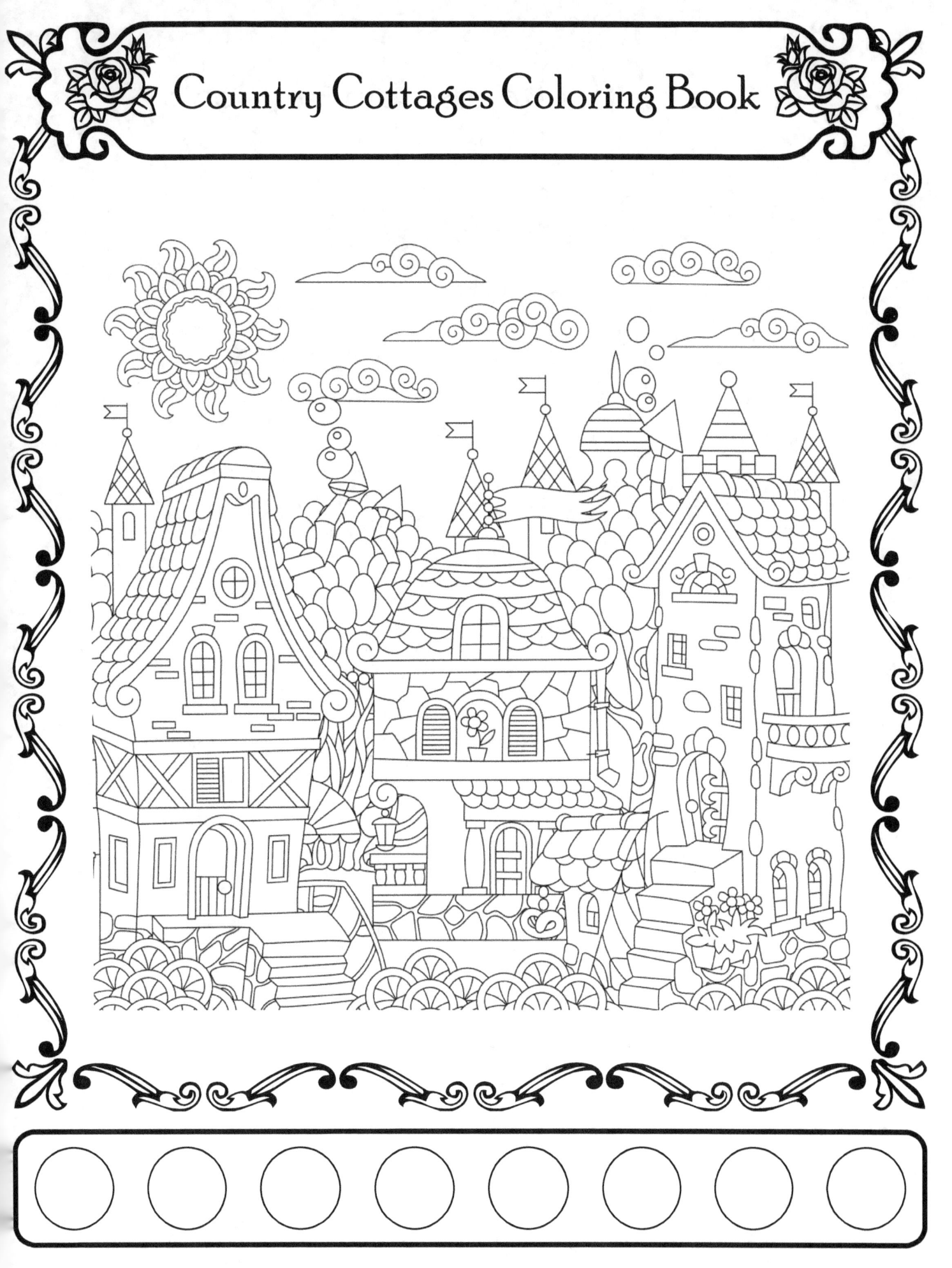

Country Cottages Coloring Book

Country Cottages Coloring Book

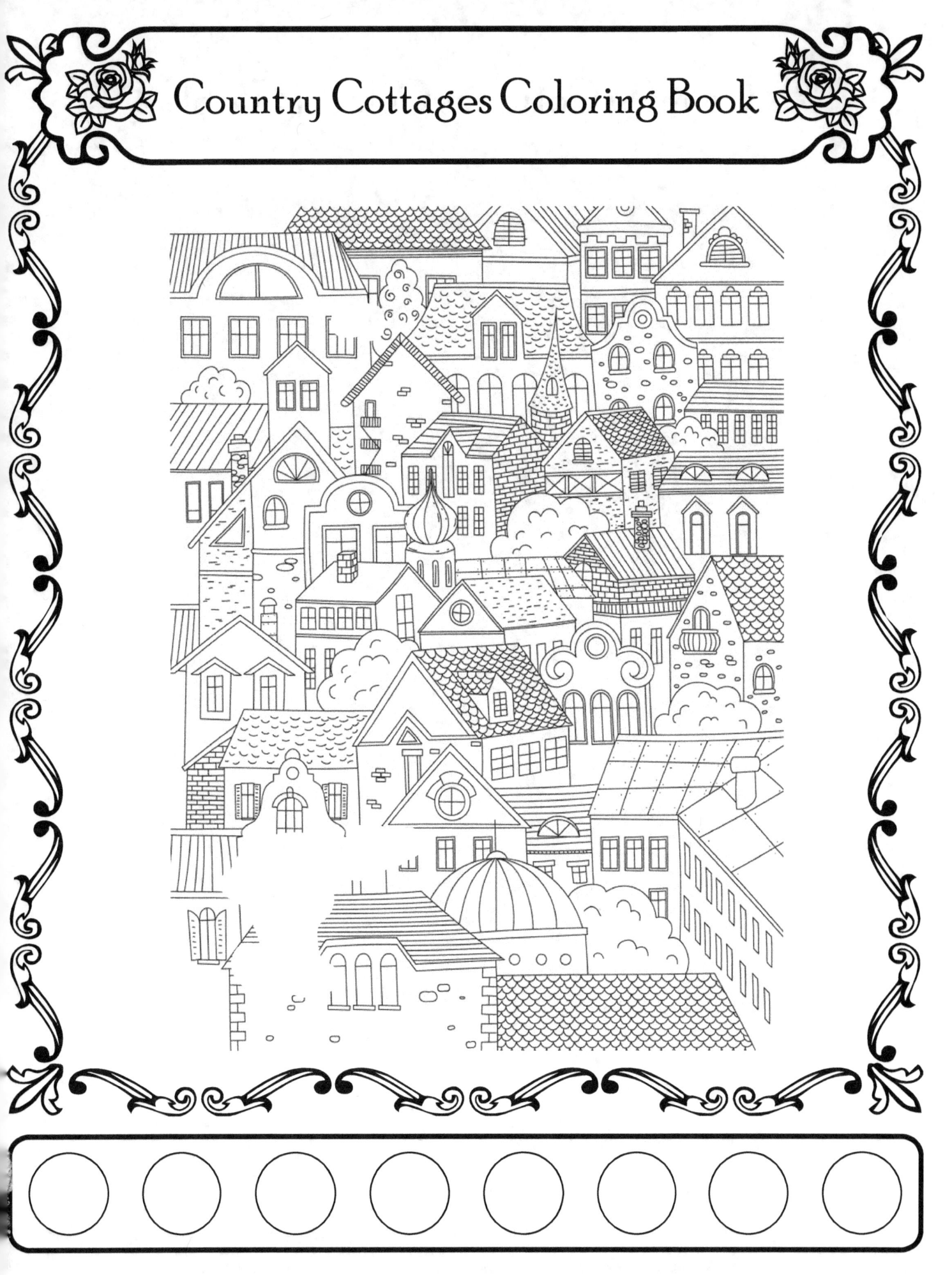

Country Cottages Coloring Book

Country Cottages Coloring Book

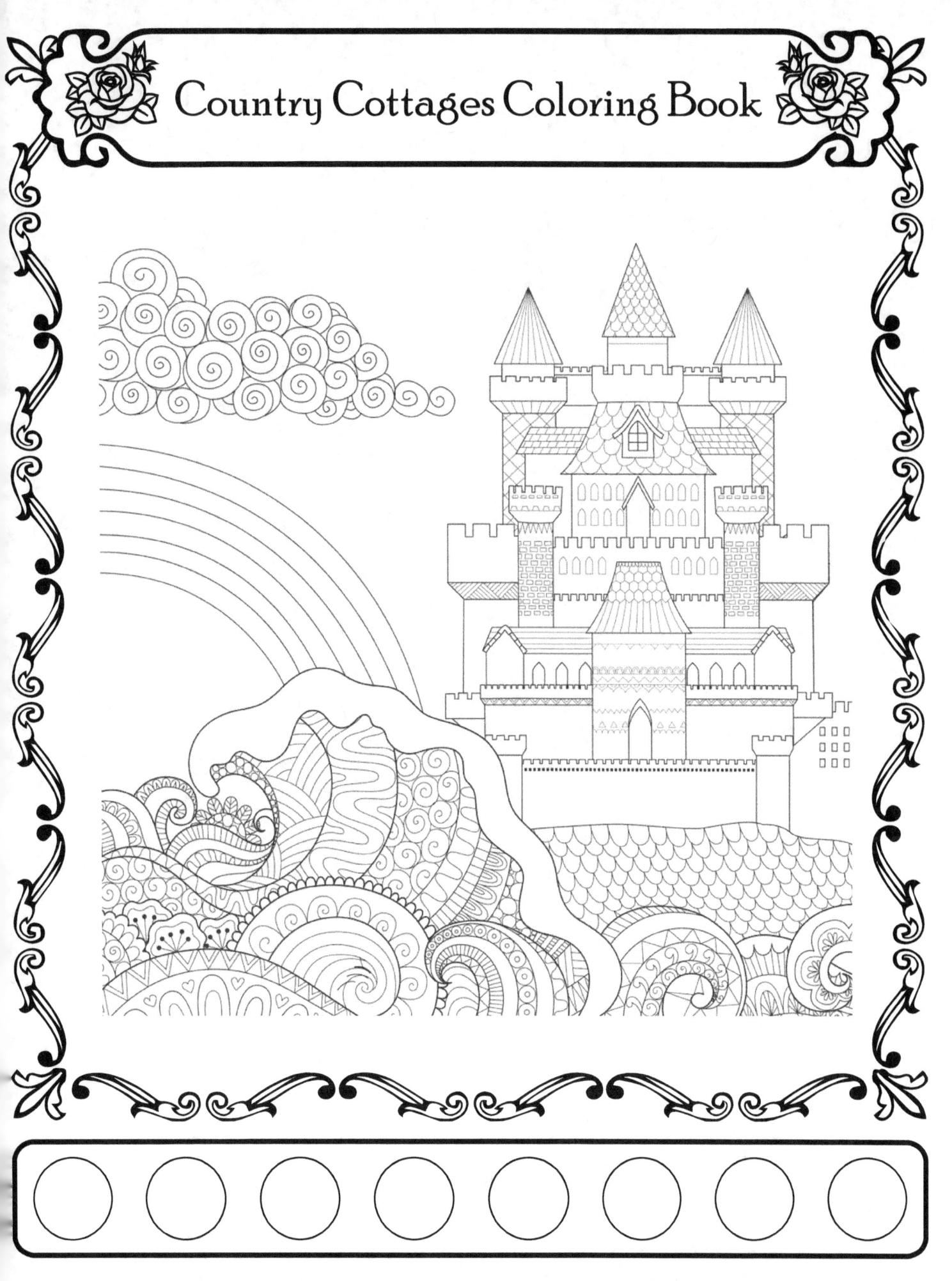

Country Cottages Coloring Book

Country Cottages Coloring Book

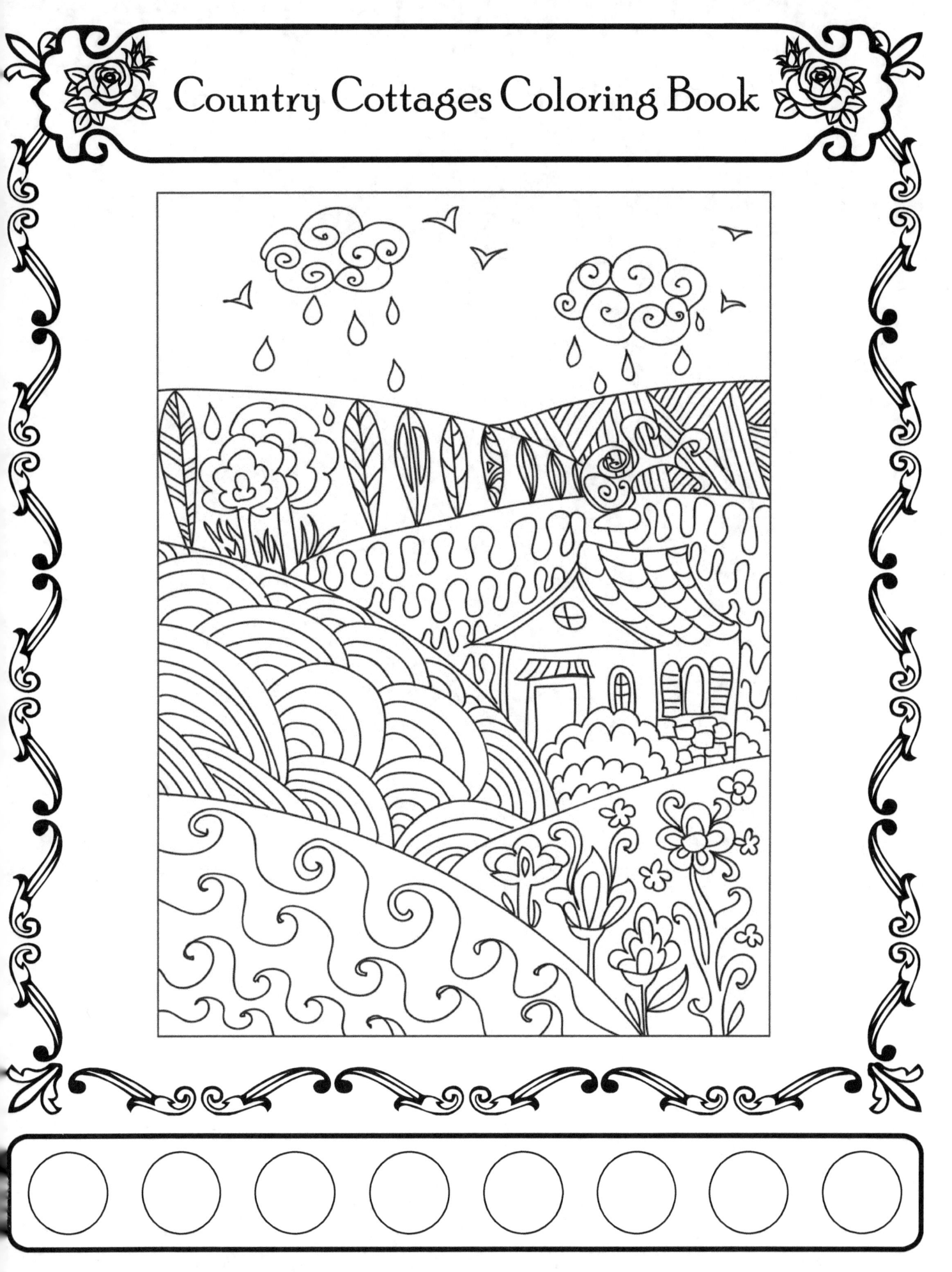

Country Cottages Coloring Book

Country Cottages Coloring Book

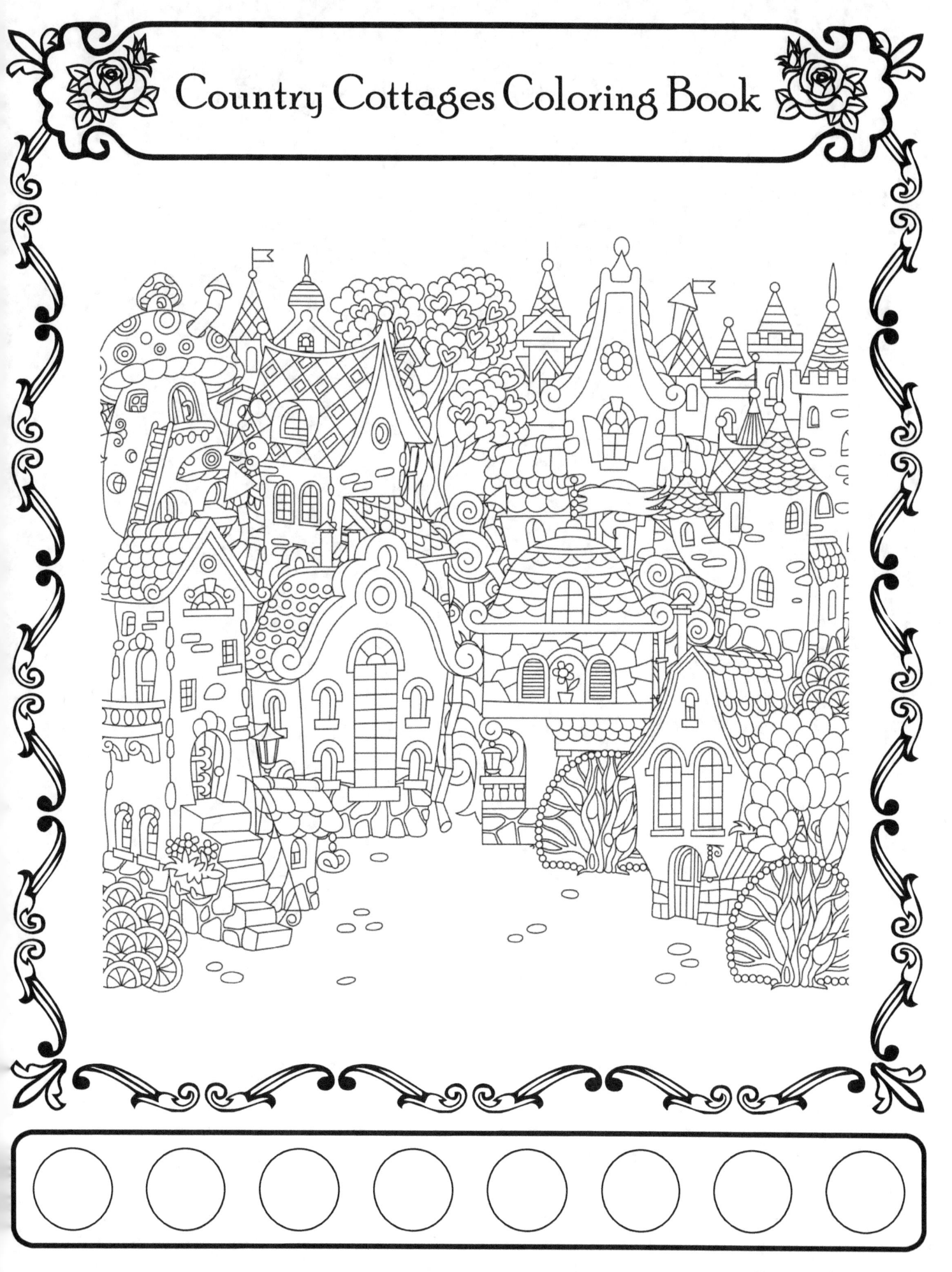

Country Cottages Coloring Book

Country Cottages Coloring Book

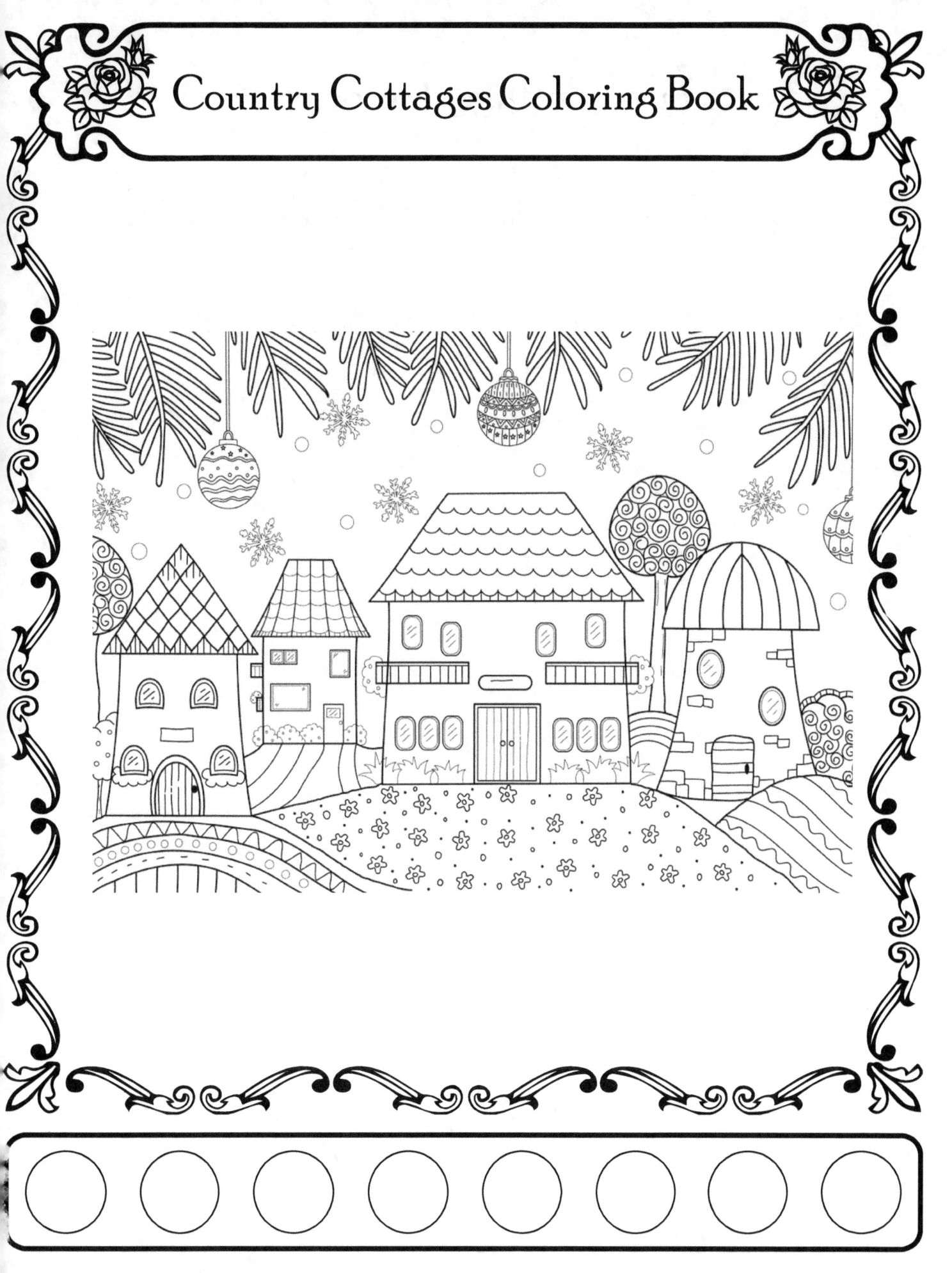

Country Cottages Coloring Book

Country Cottages Coloring Book

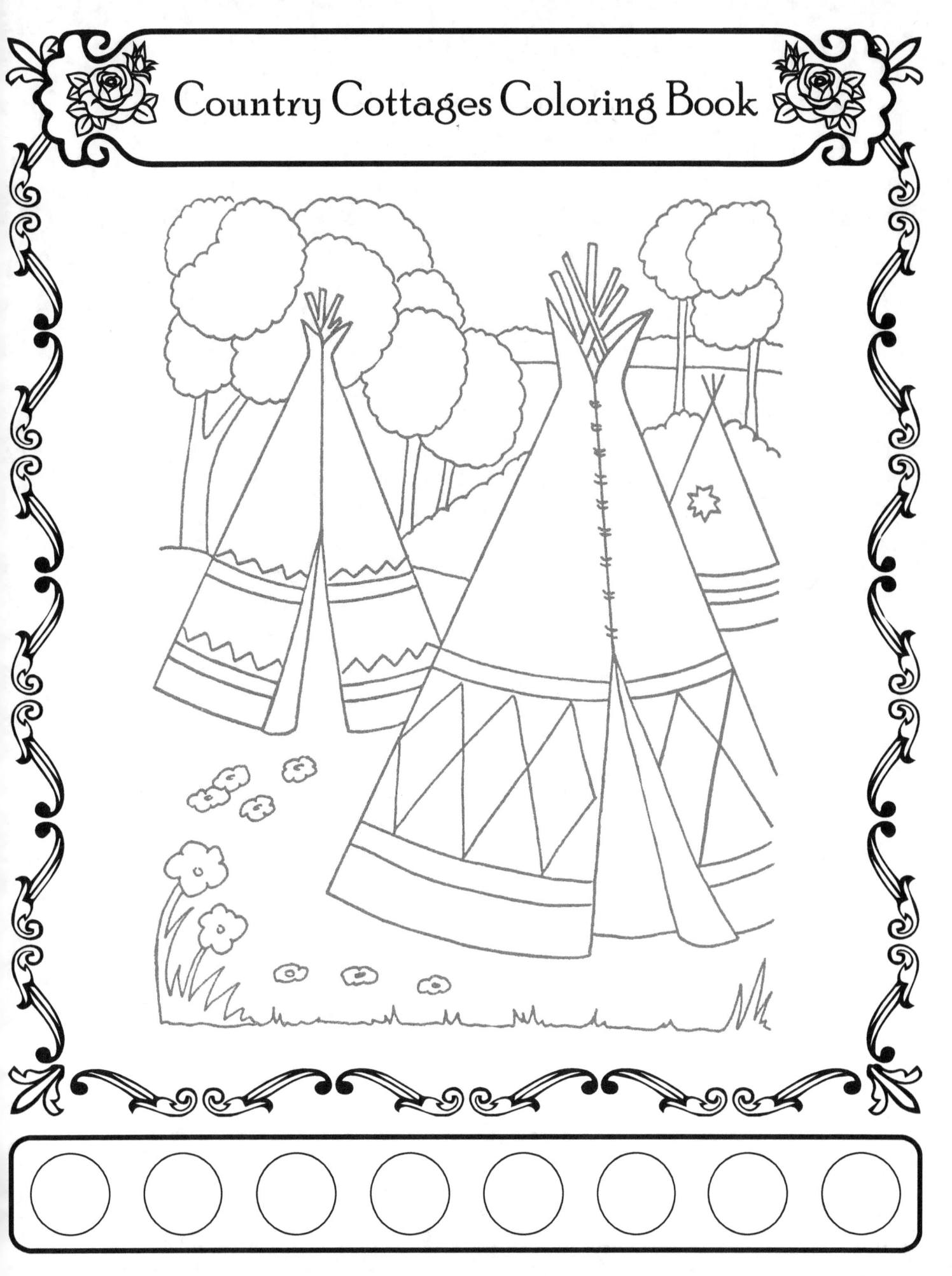

Country Cottages Coloring Book

Country Cottages Coloring Book

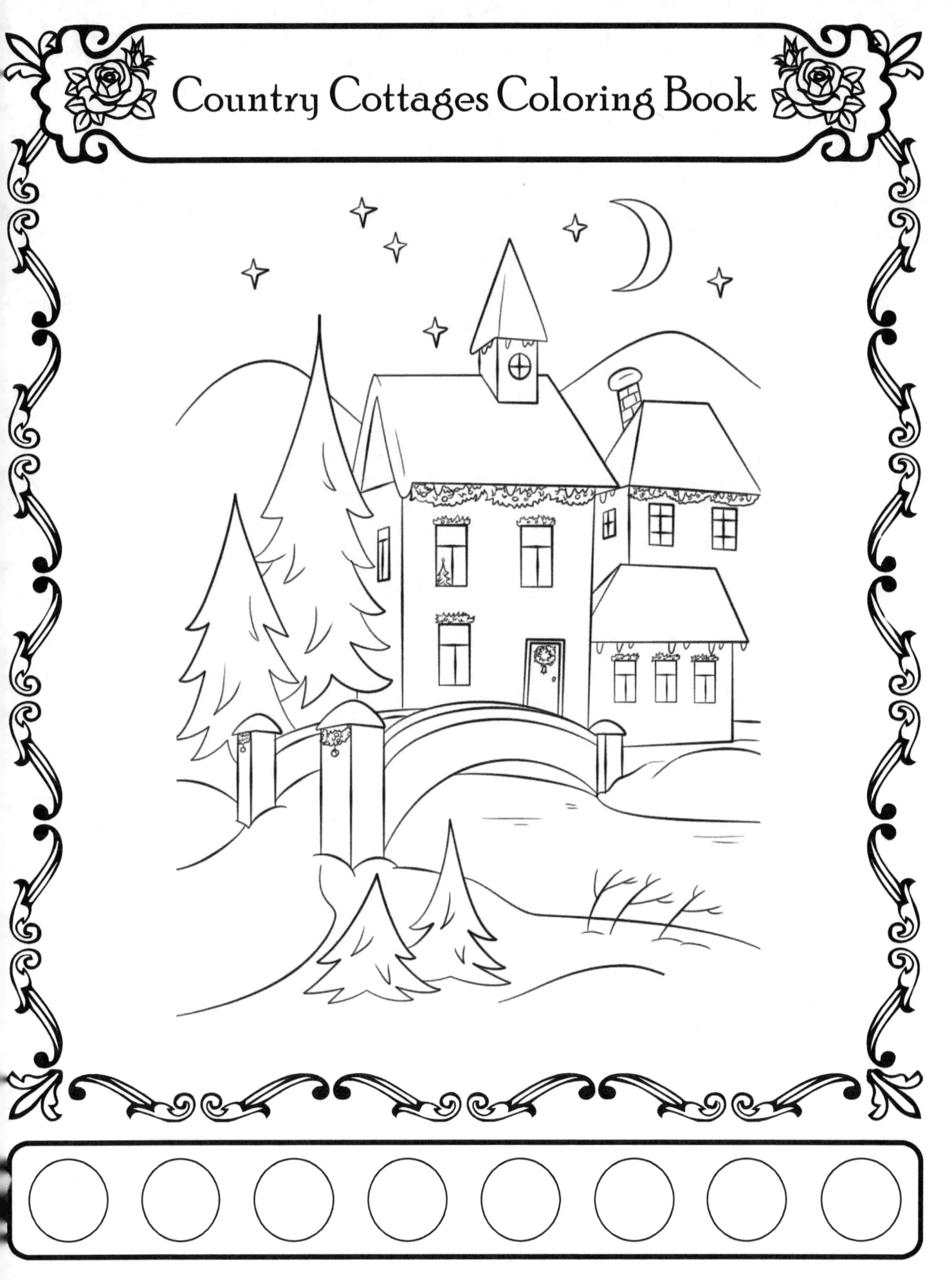

Country Cottages Coloring Book

Country Cottages Coloring Book

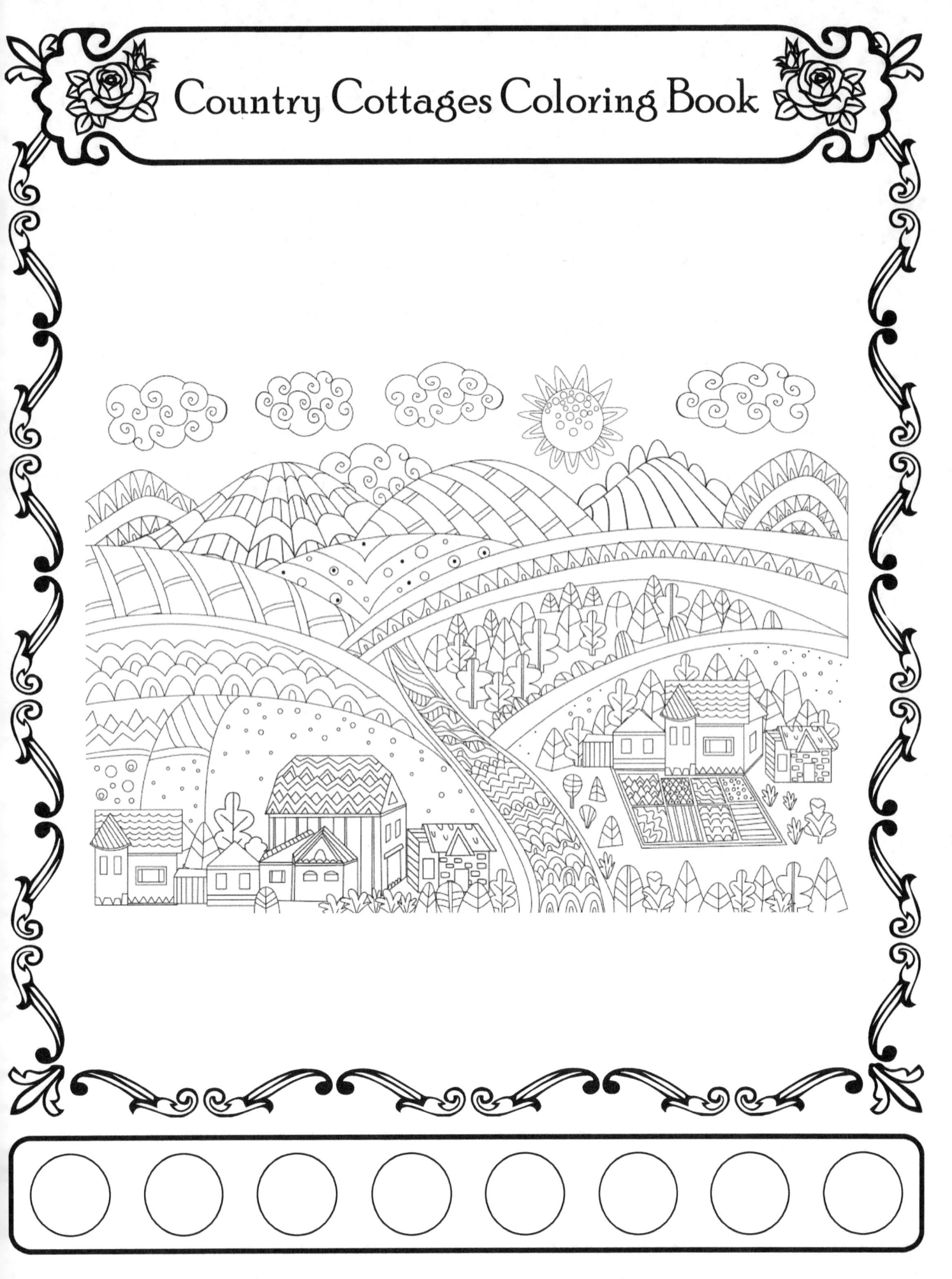

Country Cottages Coloring Book

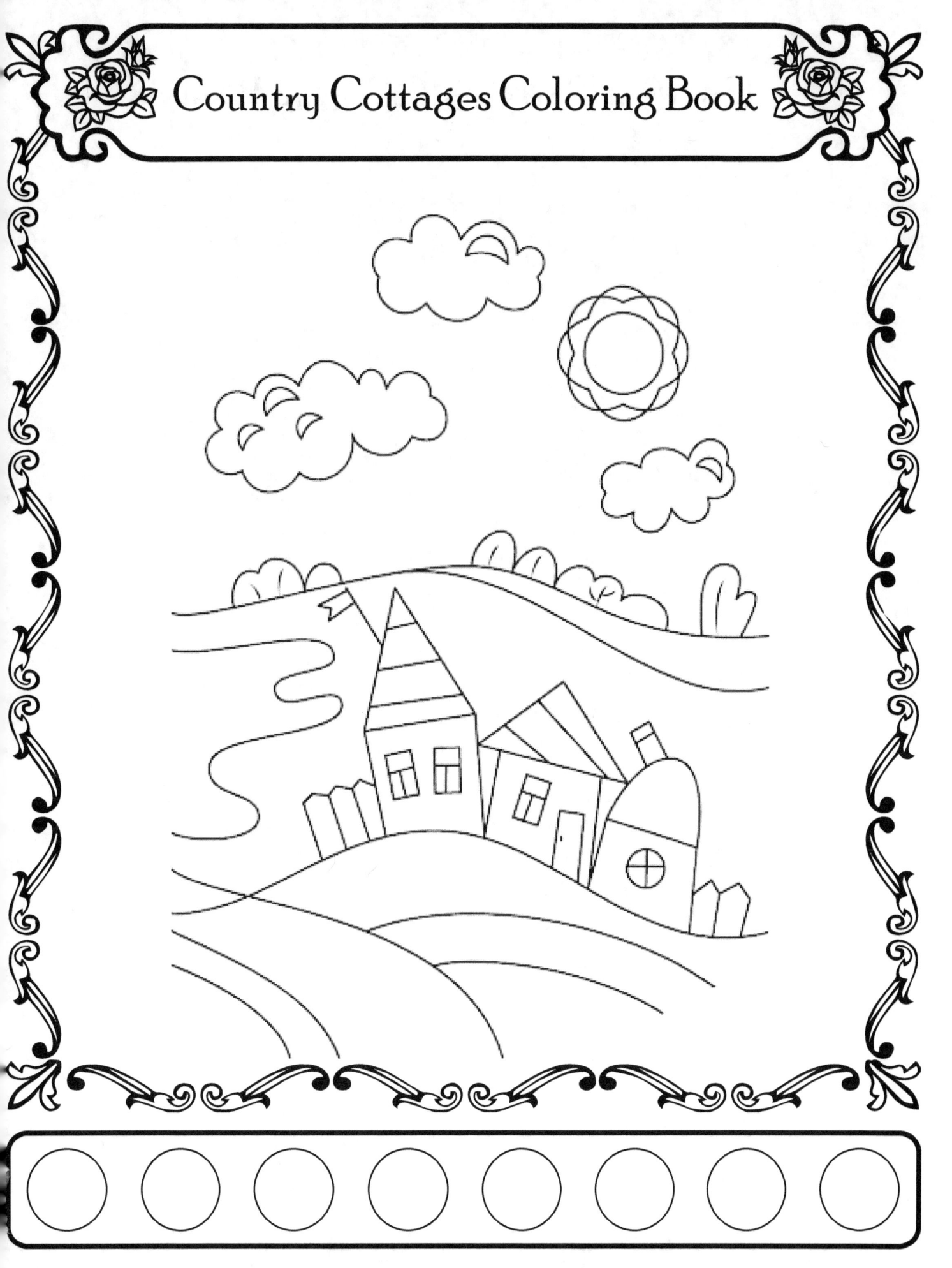

Country Cottages Coloring Book

Country Cottages Coloring Book

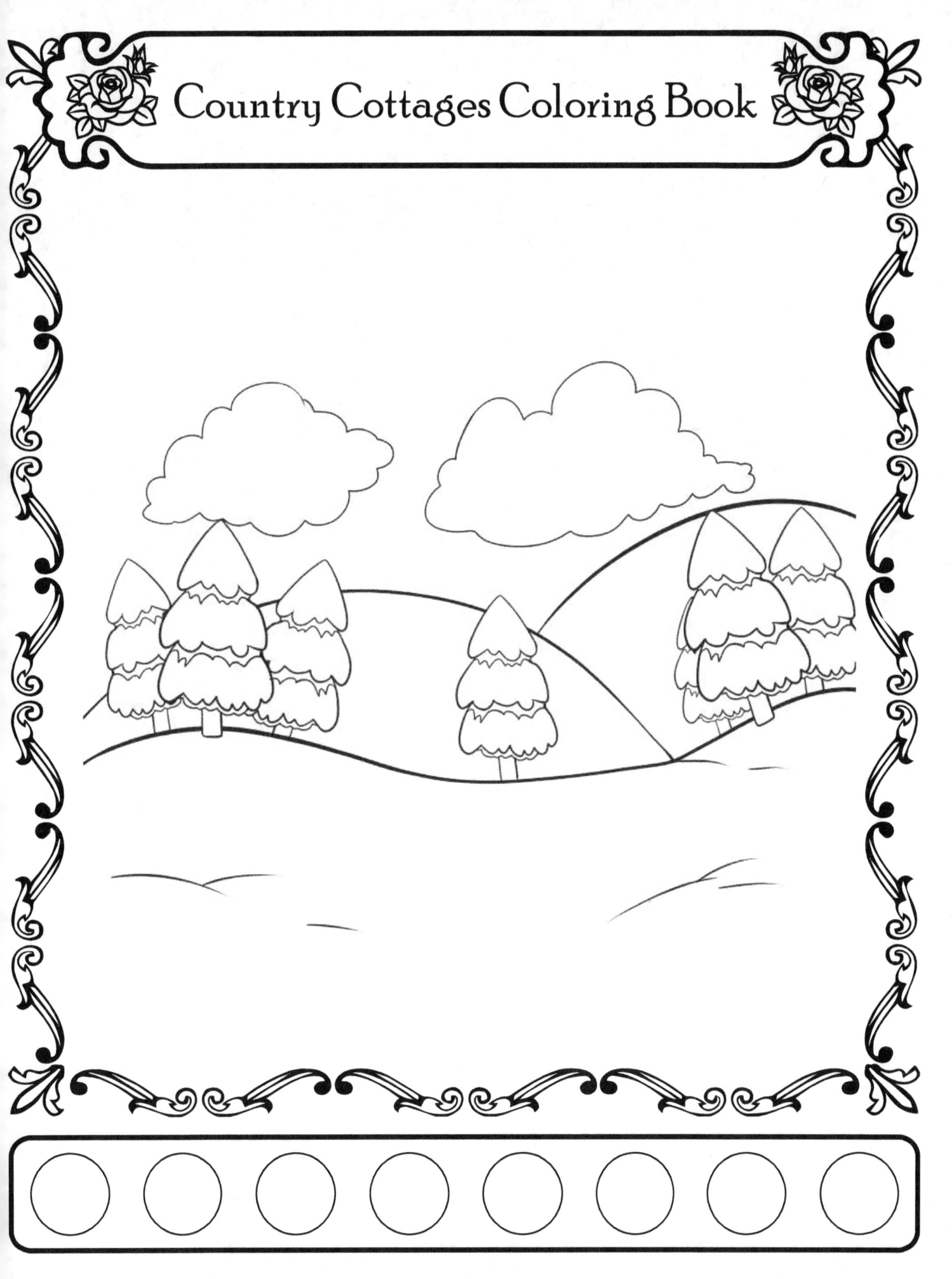

Country Cottages Coloring Book

Country Cottages Coloring Book

Country Cottages Coloring Book

Country Cottages Coloring Book

Country Cottages Coloring Book

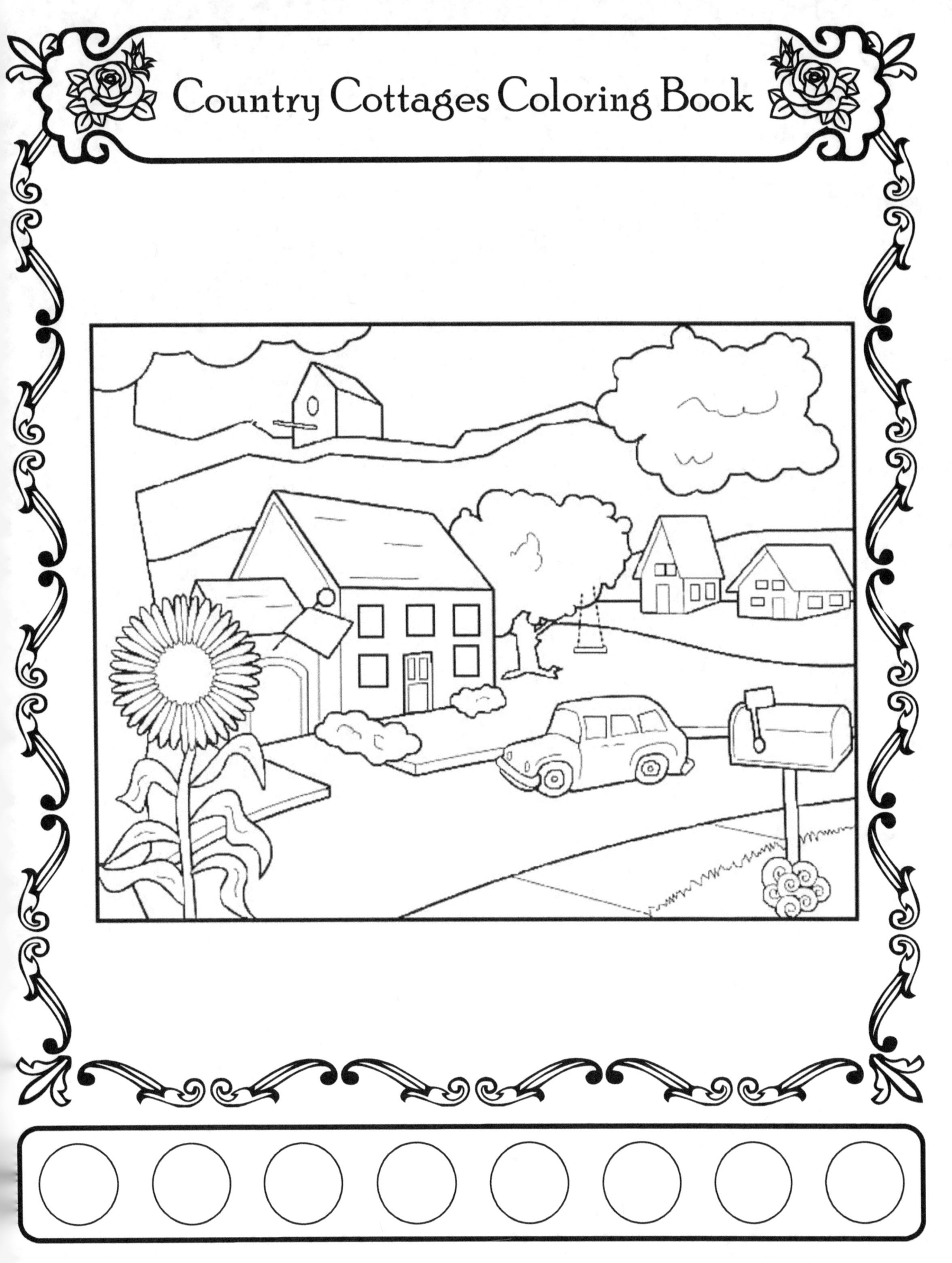

Country Cottages Coloring Book

Country Cottages Coloring Book

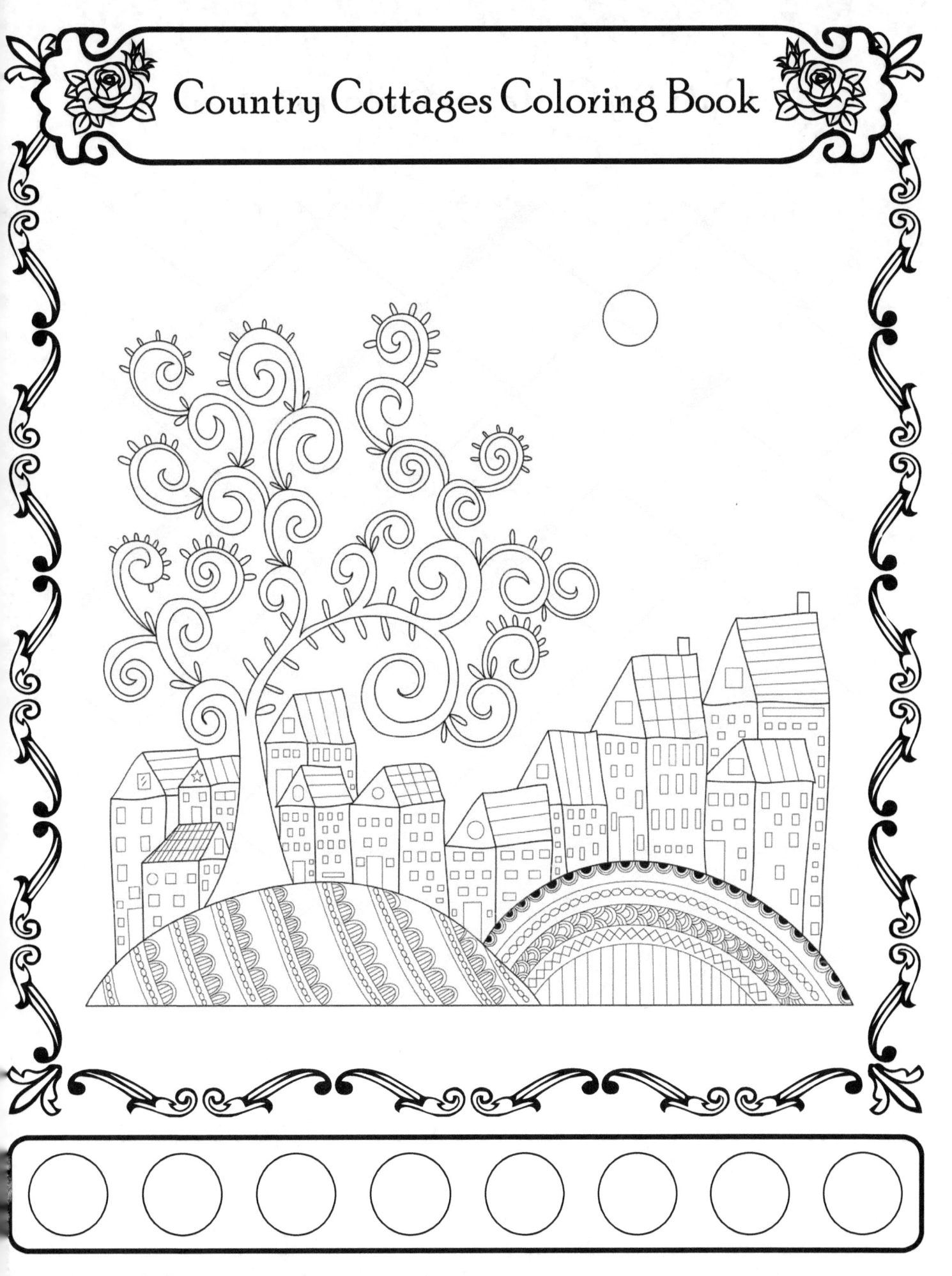

Country Cottages Coloring Book

Country Cottages Coloring Book

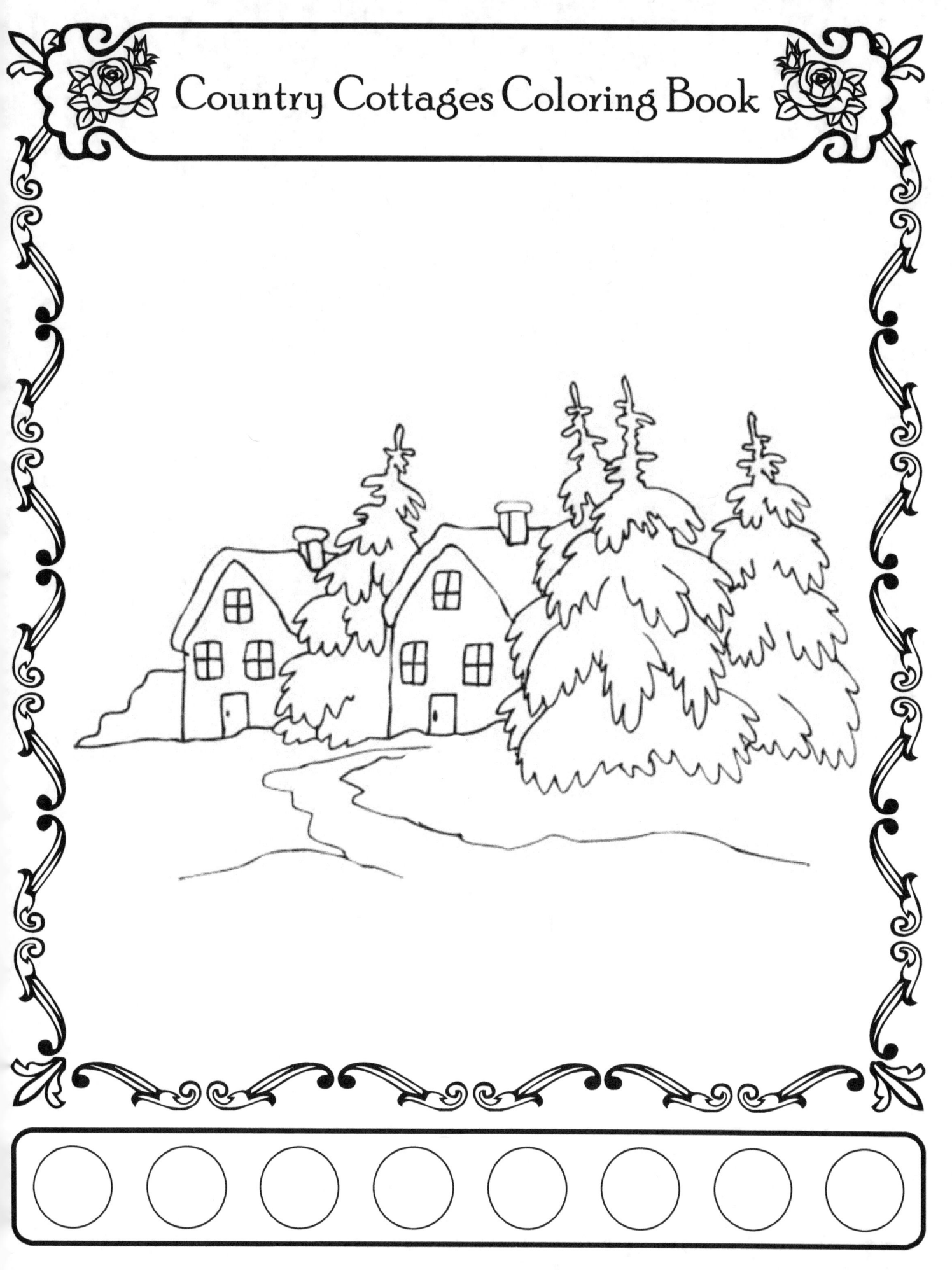

Country Cottages Coloring Book

Country Cottages Coloring Book

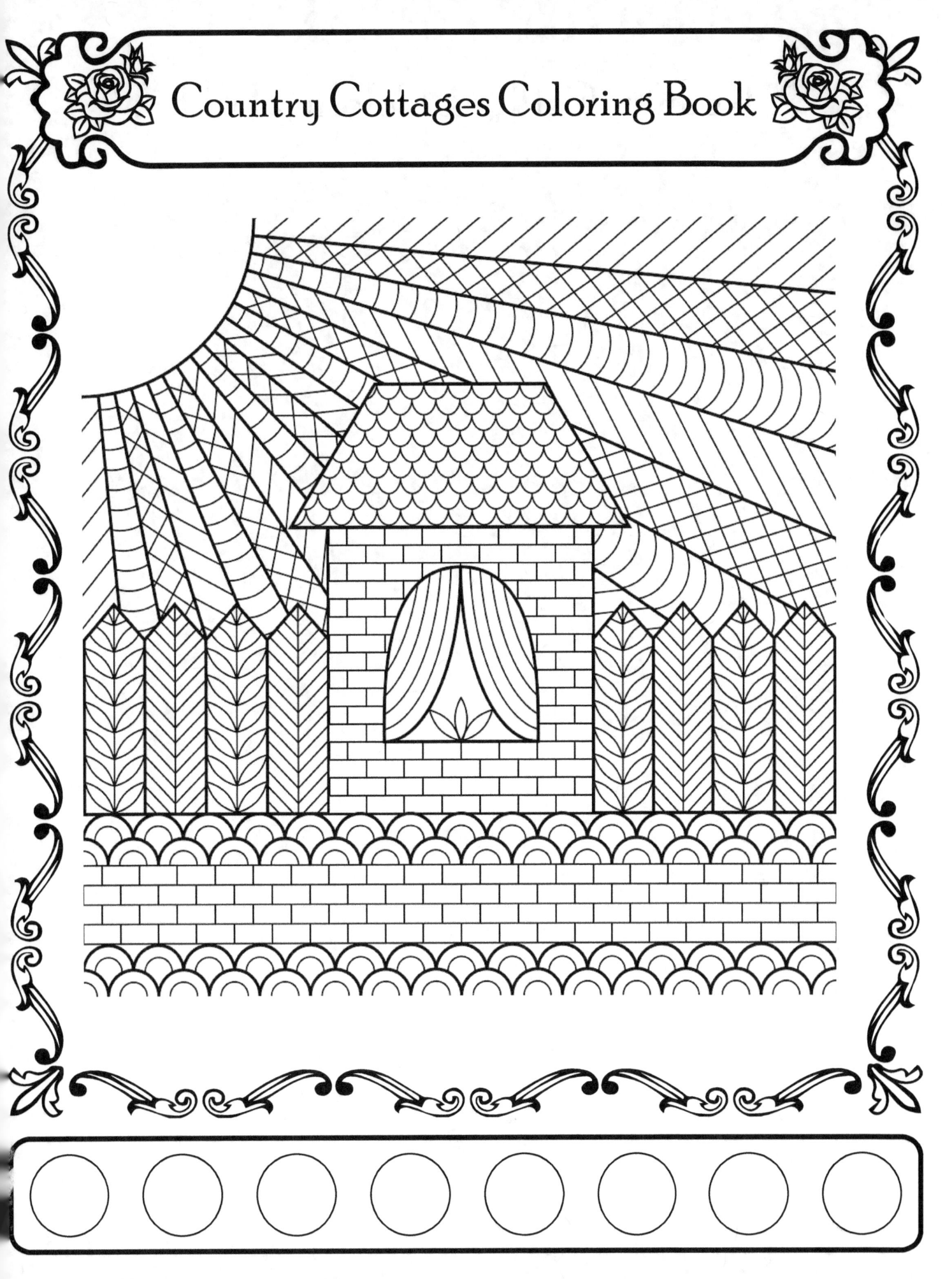

Country Cottages Coloring Book

Country Cottages Coloring Book

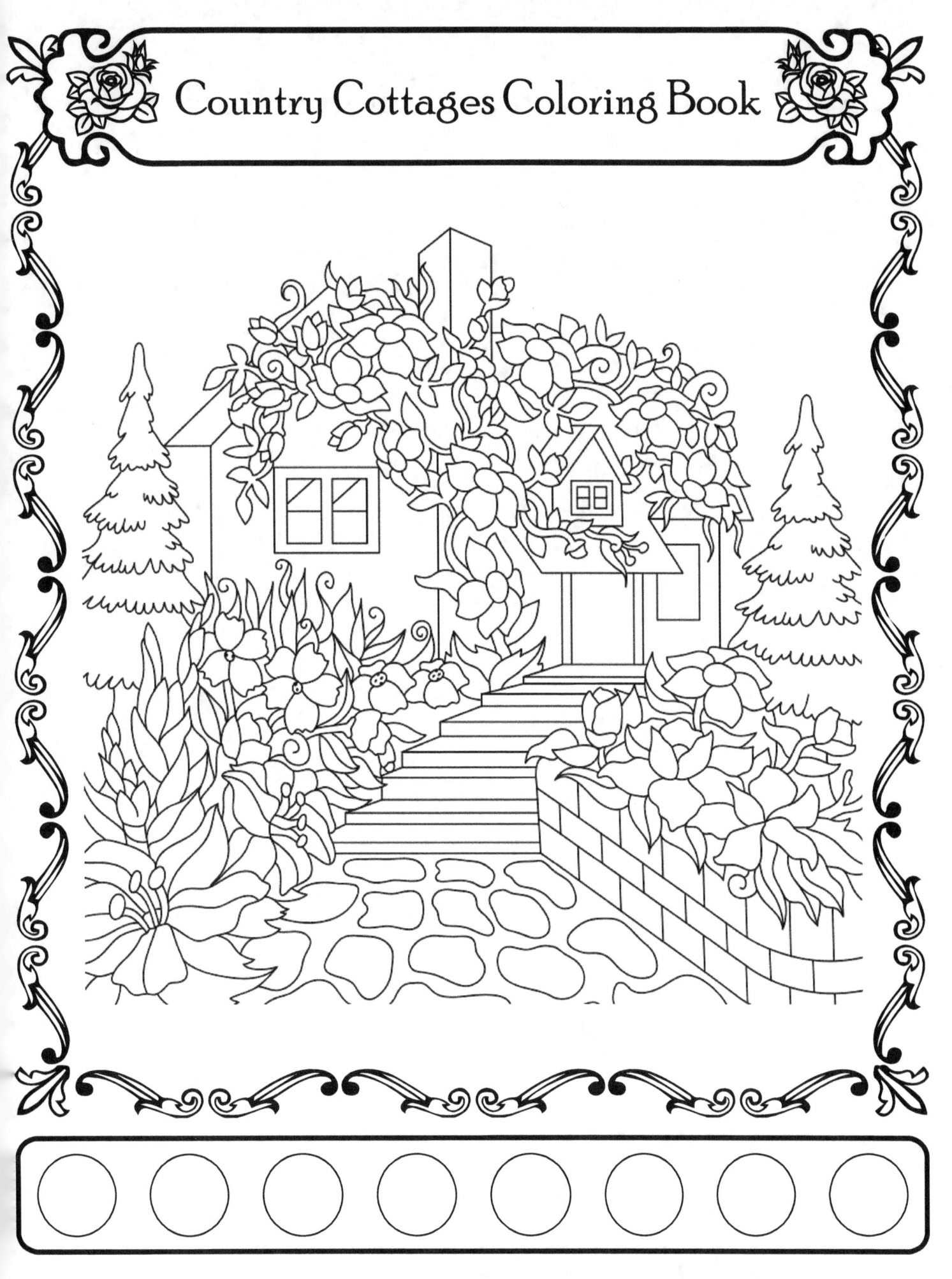

Country Cottages Coloring Book

Country Cottages Coloring Book

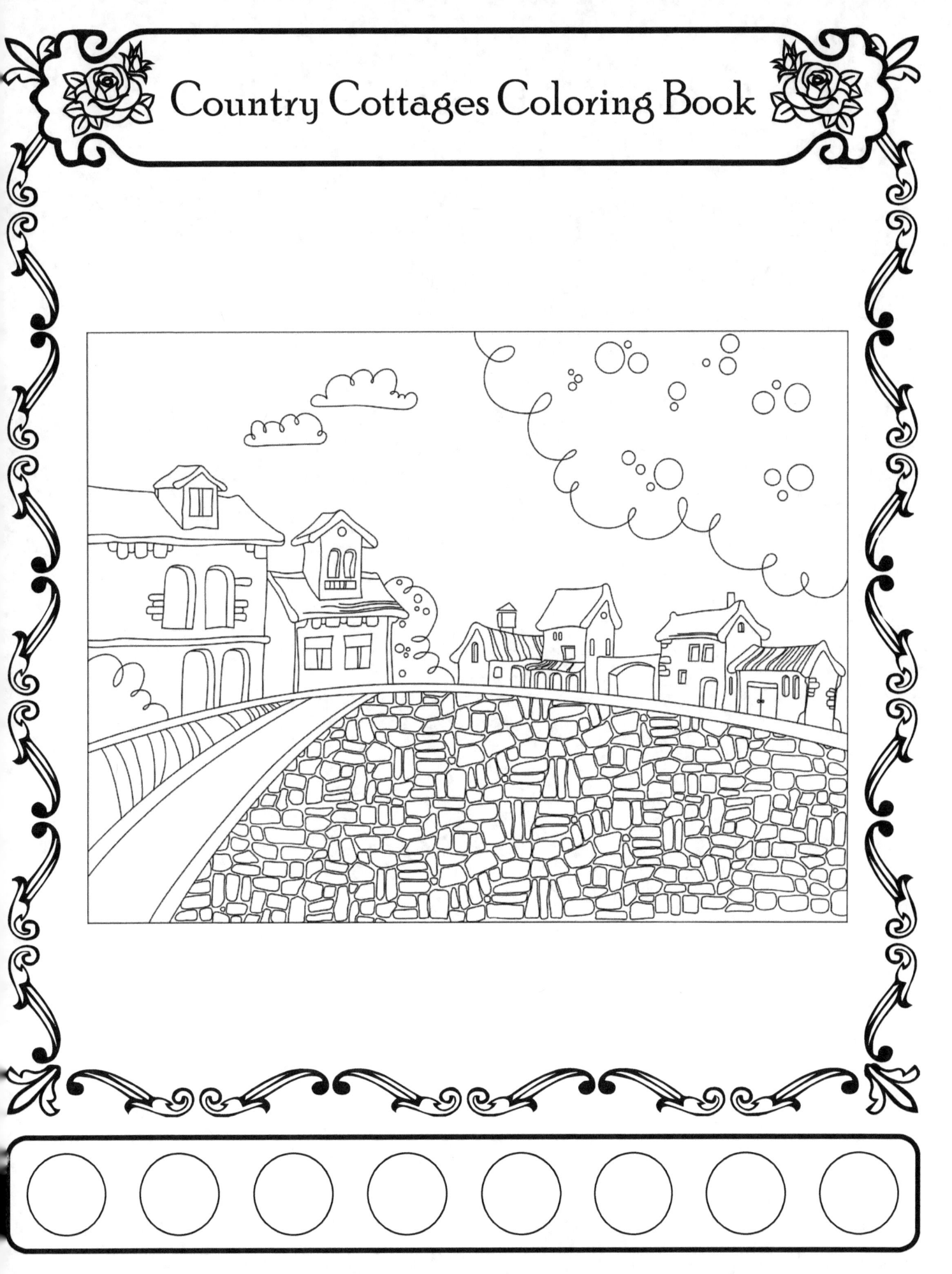

Country Cottages Coloring Book

Country Cottages Coloring Book

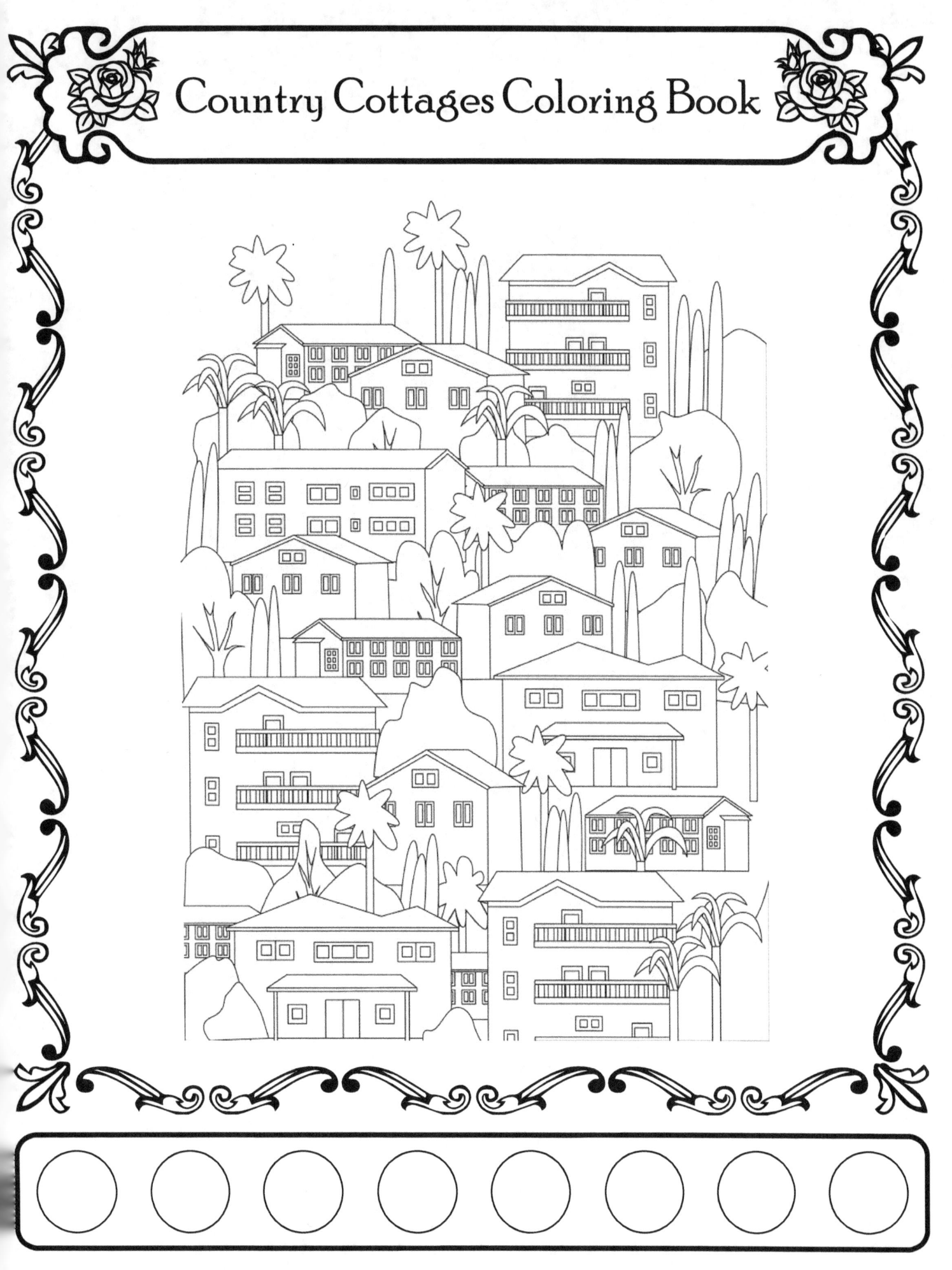

Country Cottages Coloring Book

Country Cottages Coloring Book

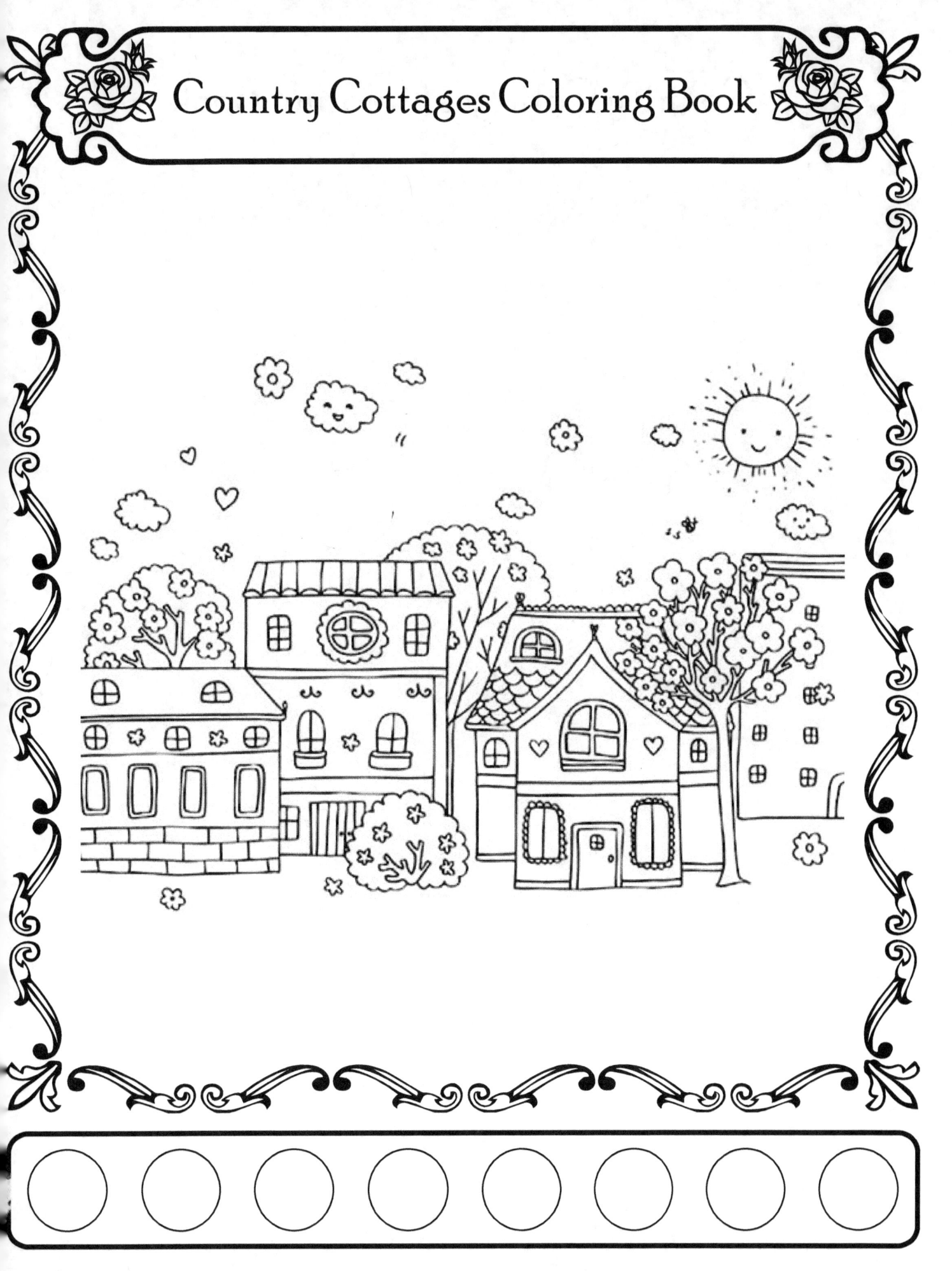

Country Cottages Coloring Book

Country Cottages Coloring Book

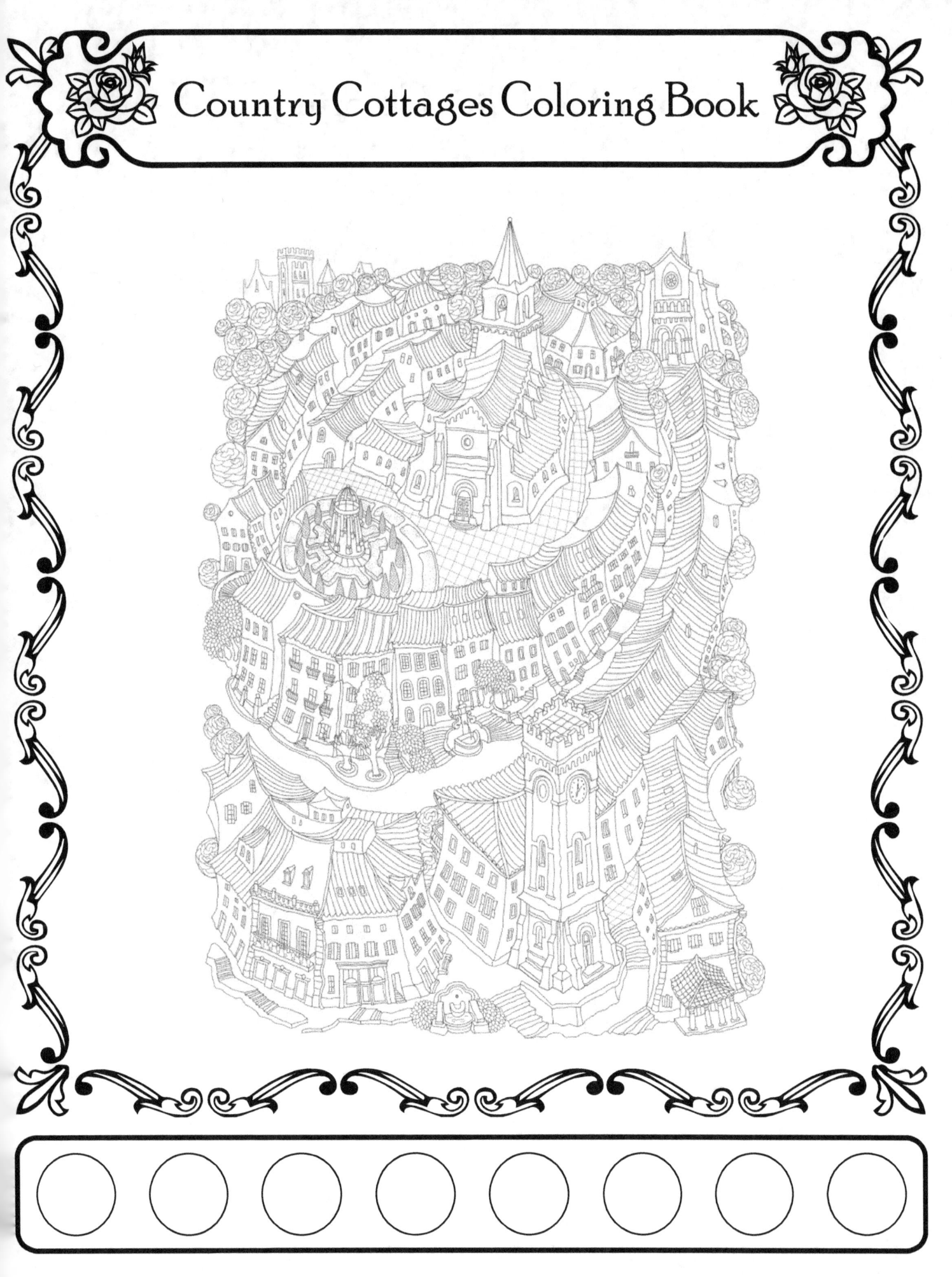

Country Cottages Coloring Book

Country Cottages Coloring Book

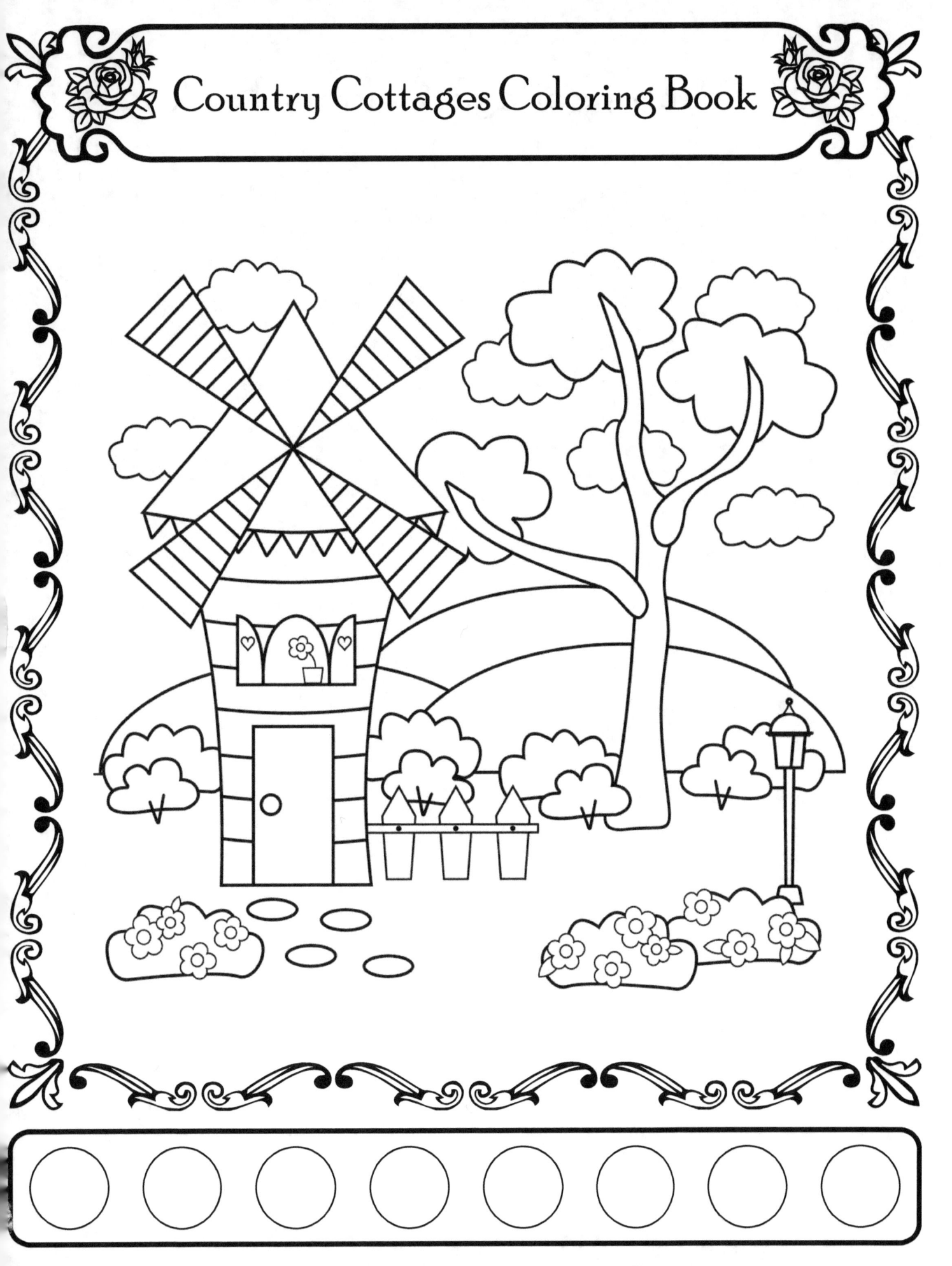

Country Cottages Coloring Book

Country Cottages Coloring Book

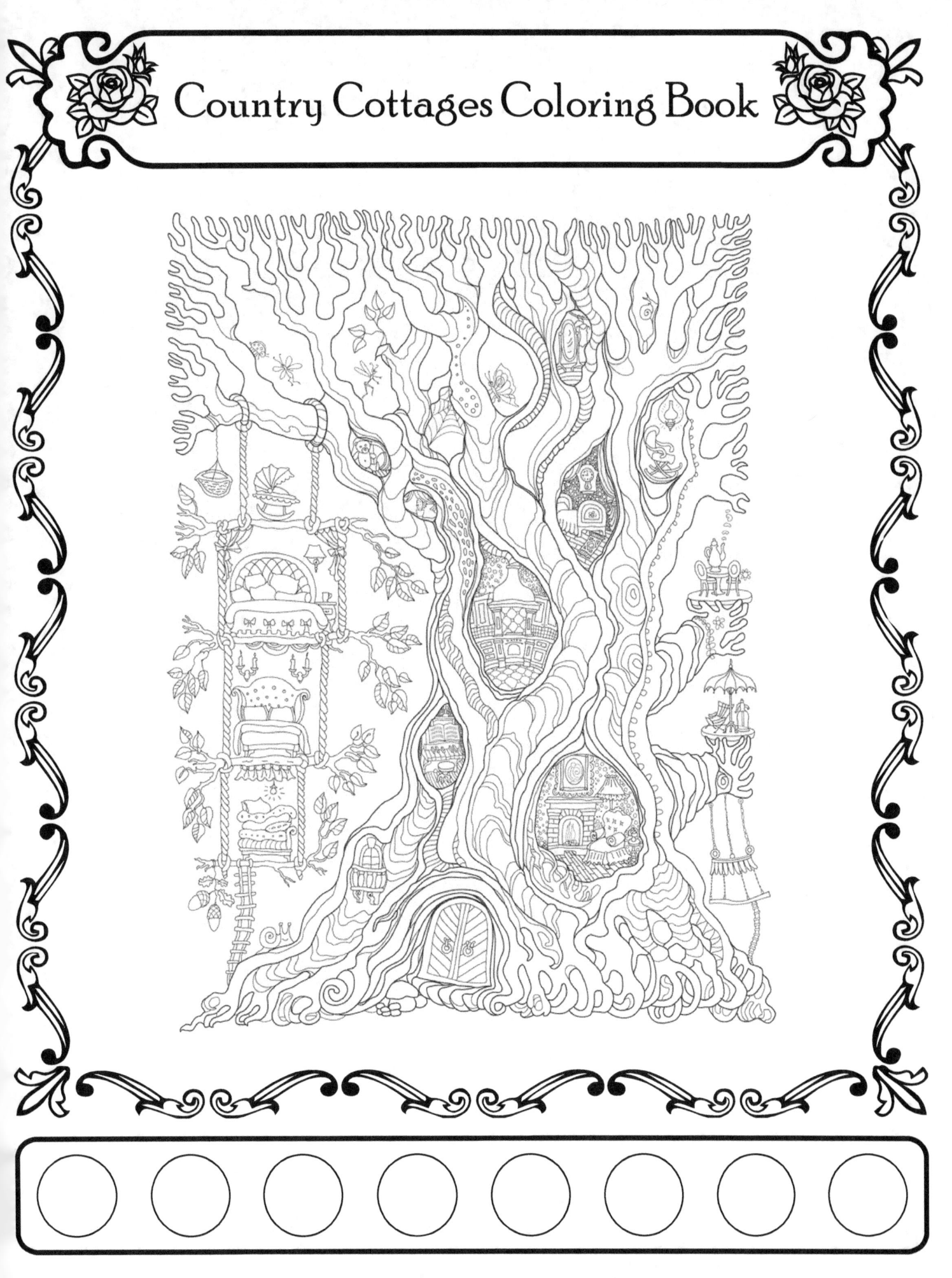

Country Cottages Coloring Book

Country Cottages Coloring Book

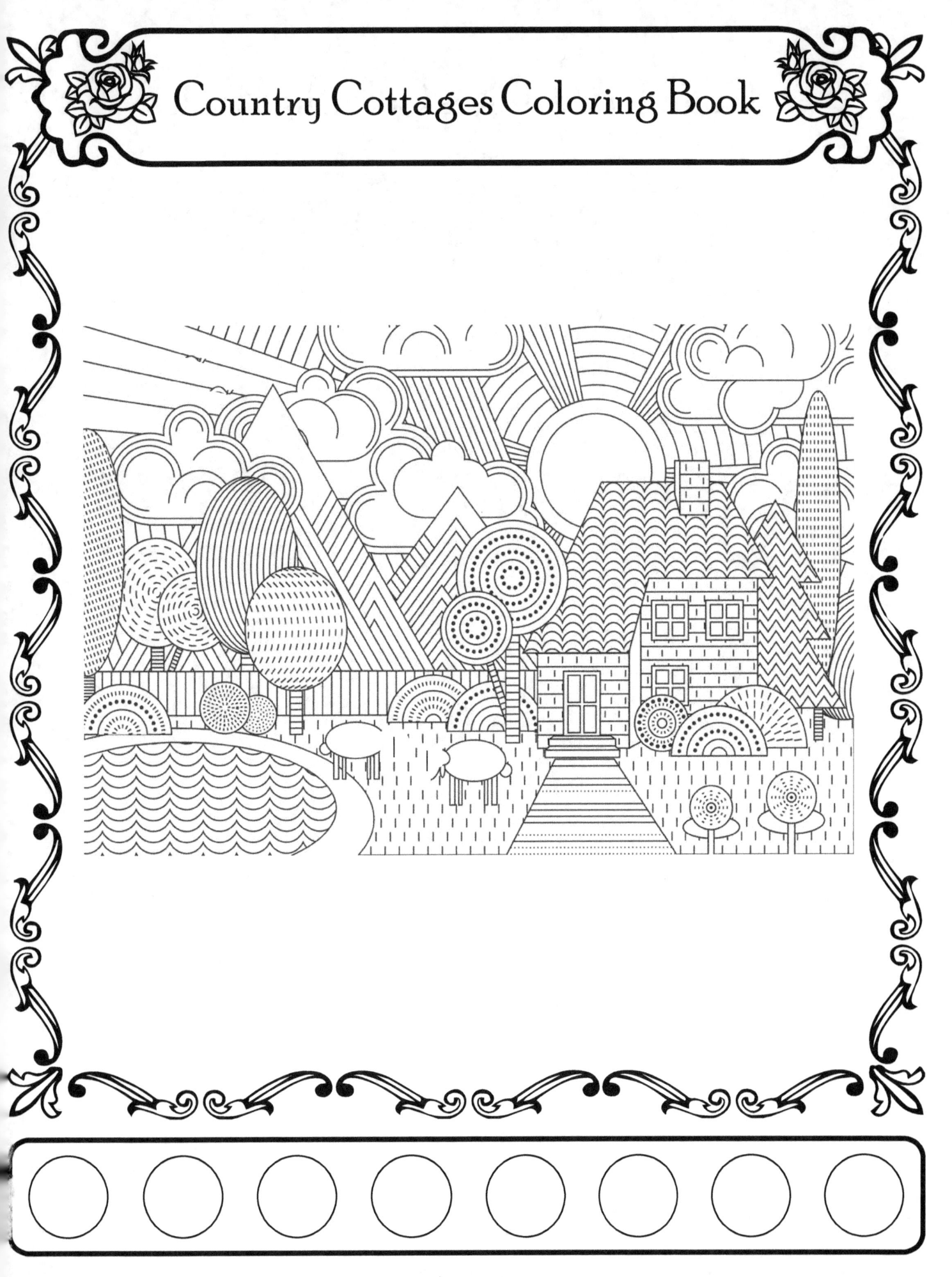

Country Cottages Coloring Book

Country Cottages Coloring Book

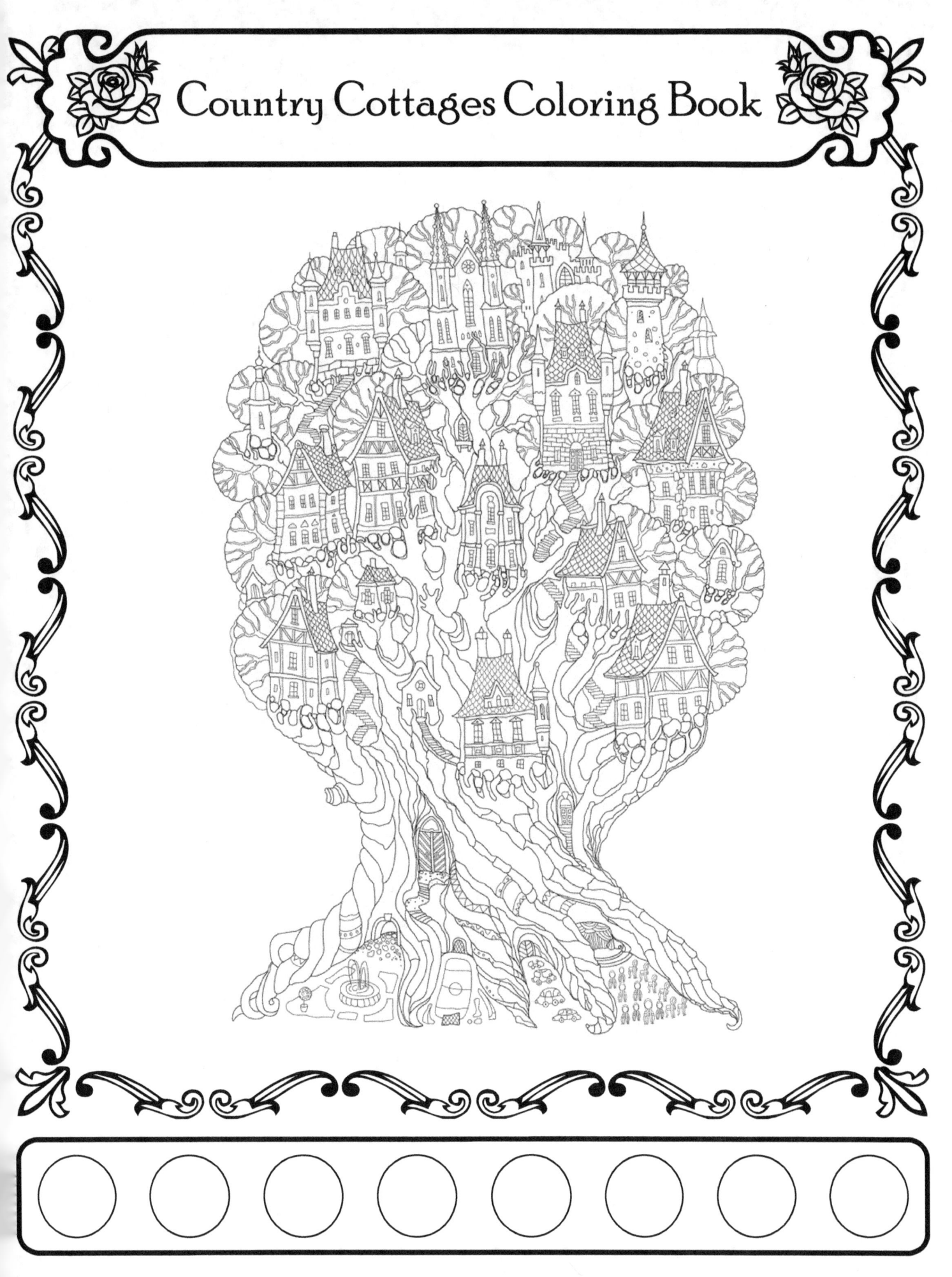

Country Cottages Coloring Book